CHAPPELL ROAN

A Little Golden Book® Biography

By Cat Reynolds

Illustrated by Maria Lia Malandrino

A GOLDEN BOOK • NEW YORK

Golden Books
An imprint of Random House Children's Books
A division of Penguin Random House LLC
1745 Broadway, New York, NY 10019
penguinrandomhouse.com
rhcbooks.com

Library of Congress Control Number: 2024949984
ISBN 979-8-217-03215-0 (trade) — ISBN 979-8-217-03216-7 (ebook)
Manufactured in the United States of America
10 9 8 7 6 5 4 3 2
EU Contact: Penguin Random House Ireland, 32 Nassau Street, Dublin D02 YH68.
https://eu-contact.penguin.ie

On February 19, 1998, in the small town of Willard, Missouri, Kayleigh Rose Amstutz was born. Someday, the world would know her as Chappell Roan, the pop star. But for now, she was Kayleigh, the oldest child of Kara and Dwight, a veterinarian and a nurse.

Ever since she was a little girl, Kayleigh loved music. She enjoyed singing and began taking piano lessons when she was twelve years old.

In eighth grade, Kayleigh sang "The Christmas Song" at her school's talent show. It was her first time performing for an audience. Everyone was blown away by her amazing voice. She won first place!

She auditioned for *America's Got Talent* when she was fourteen years old. She wasn't picked to be on the show, but that didn't stop Kayleigh from deciding she would be a singer when she grew up.

Kayleigh started writing her own songs. She was inspired by all kinds of music, from 1970s rock to gospel hymns. She began posting videos of herself singing on YouTube. It wasn't long before producers from a big record company noticed her talent and signed her to a deal. Kayleigh was only seventeen years old.

It was hard starting her music career while still in high school. She had to fly to New York City and Los Angeles often. Kayleigh missed out on going to prom and graduation, but her dreams were coming true.

She decided to use a stage name and chose one to honor her grandfather, Dennis Chappell. "The Strawberry Roan" was the name of his favorite old Western song. That's how Kayleigh Rose Amstutz became Chappell Roan!

In 2017, Chappell released her first single. It was a sad, slow song that she cowrote. The following year, she moved to Los Angeles full-time. The record company wanted more songs just like her first one, but living away from home taught Chappell a lot about herself. She didn't think that first song reflected who she was anymore. She wanted to write different music.

She wrote an upbeat ballad called "Pink Pony Club" with her friend and producer Dan Nigro. Chappell was proud of the new song and felt like it came from her heart. Even though the record company wasn't sure they liked the song's style, they released it in 2020.

When "Pink Pony Club" wasn't popular right away, the record company decided to stop working with Chappell. She was disappointed, but if she was going to be a musician, she wanted to make music that *she* loved.

Chappell moved back home to Missouri, where she worked as a barista at a drive-through coffee shop while she continued to write new songs.

During that time, something amazing happened: "Pink Pony Club" became more and more popular every day! It seemed that people really liked listening to the music that Chappell liked creating. After just a couple of months in Missouri, Chappell moved back to Los Angeles to give her dream another shot.

Chappell started writing and releasing new music as an independent artist. Her new songs were all about being yourself and loving who you want to love. She continued to work with Dan. She made her own music videos with the help of her friends. She taught herself how to bedazzle costumes and apply big, bold makeup.

Chappell's first album, *The Rise and Fall of a Midwest Princess*, came out in 2023. It was a hit! Before she knew it, she was giving concerts around the world and singing on TV!

At her concerts, Chappell's fans discovered that she's not only an incredible singer and songwriter, she's also an amazing performer! She does splits, flips her big red hair, tells stories to the audience, and even teaches them dance moves. Her fans love dancing along with her!

HOT TO GO!

Chappell enjoys wearing whimsical outfits and over-the-top makeup.

You never know where she might find inspiration:
an old prom dress, a football jersey, a swan queen, even
the Statue of Liberty!

Chappell encourages her fans to dress up, too. She gives her concerts a theme, like mermaids or rainbows, and asks people to wear whatever makes them feel happy. Dressing up together is a fun way for Chappell to connect with her fans!

Helping others is very important to Chappell.
She donates a portion of ticket sales to organizations that
provide support to people in the LGBTQ+ community. In
every city she visits, she asks local drag queens to perform
before her shows. Chappell knows everyone should have
equal rights, no matter who they are or who they love.

In 2024, Chappell performed for huge crowds at major music festivals across the country. Due to her popularity, some festivals moved her act to a bigger stage so more people could see her. And she set a record for the biggest crowd ever at Lollapalooza!

A month later, Chappell attended the MTV Video Music Awards for the first time. She performed her hit song "Good Luck, Babe!" and won the award for Best New Artist! In 2025, Chappell was named Best New Artist again, this time at the Grammy Awards!

Chappell faced many challenges over the years, but she never gave up on her dream. Being true to herself and creating the music she loves has made Chappell Roan the artist she is today. Her songs bring joy to her fans, reminding them that they deserve to be accepted exactly as they are. And that brings joy to Chappell.